NATIONAL GEOGRAPHIC

D0602863

Look at the Leaves

Rachel Griffiths

You can sort the leaves by **color**.

You can sort the leaves by **size**.

5

You can sort the leaves by **shape**.

How would you sort the leaves?